Mary Towneley Loop

A Pocket Guide

Please note:
Some riders have found problems negotiating horse stiles on the Loop, particularly with young horses.
If you aren't sure if your horse will step calmly through them we strongly advise you to practice at home, as there is no way around some of them on the Loop.
Please be prepared for all eventualities and carry phone numbers such as your B&B provider.
You will need to give a grid reference and location if you need emergency assistance so ensure you have a map with you and know how to use it.
It is also recommended that you carry a basic first aid kit and waterproof clothing at all times.
On the section between Waterfoot and Deerplay there are a lot of gates.
Being able to open and close them from your horse can save a lot of time and effort.

The Forest of Rossendale Bridleways Association

The Forest of Rossendale Bridleway Ass was formed in 1980 by a group of riders who wanted a better deal on rights of way. Rossendale has 404 miles of rights of way with only 22 miles available to horse riders. Over the years the group has raised money through subscriptions, rides and events to provide funds for reclaiming and improving rights of way. The first edition of the "The Mary Towneley Loop – A Pocket Guide" has raised as much again and is being used for research to upgrade routes to their correct status.

Chris Peat has been involved with FORBA since its conception. The group has an active calendar of monthly rides and social events. Promoting safe and responsible riding wherever it takes place remains paramount.

FORBA or Chris can be contacted at
www.forba.org.uk   mail@chrispeat.co.uk   01254 386459

South Pennine Packhorse Trails Trust

The South Pennine Packhorse Trails Trust was established in 1989 and since then has raised and invested over £500,000 in bridleway restoration work, from research through to the work on the ground. During this time 68 miles of bridleways and byways have had their status secured, and over 62 miles of bridleways and byways have been improved. Guide books about the trails published by the Trust are available. With your help more could be done –contact SPPTT on 01706 815598.

Glen Valley Guest House

Set in the quiet village of Waterfoot, Glen Valley Guesthouse, a registered member of Lancashire and Blackpool tourist board, is within easy proximity to The Mary Towneley Loop section of The Pennine Bridleway.

In conjunction with a local farm, we are offering overnight stays at Glen Valley Guesthouse with overnight livery at the farm, which includes wagon and trailer parking, 10 x12 boxes straw, shavings, hay/haylage and  transfers to and from the livery to your accommodation. There is also a local blacksmith on call and arena available upon request.

Your overnight stay at Glen Valley Guesthouse includes a full English breakfast, tea and coffee refreshment tray in your room, and combi TV/DVD for your relaxation. Also, whilst visiting the area, why not sit down to your evening meal at the local village pub, The Duke of Buccleugh, where a good variety menu is served up until 9pm.

All this is included in the price from as little as £60.00 per night We can also offer a freshly made packed lunch, available upon request from only £4.00.

**Telephone
01706 222637 or
07787904225
ask Bryan or Andy
for details.**

Pennine Bridleway

The Mary Towneley Loop

A pocket guide

Chris Peat

Maps by John B. Taylor

Designed by Wendy Taylor

Forest of Rossendale Bridleways Association

Published by the Forest of Rossendale Bridleways Association
c/o 2 Baxenden House, Manchester Road
Baxenden, Accrington. BB5 2RU

Printed in Great Britain by
rapspiderweb colour printers ltd
Clowes Street, Hollinwood, Oldham OL9 7LY

ISBN 0-9547813-0-9

Contents

*This book is dedicated to the memory of Mary Towneley,
without whom the Pennine Bridleway would not have happened,
and who sadly died before it was officially opened*

Introduction

Why do we need a pocket guide to the Mary Towneley Loop? After all, the Pennine Bridleway is signposted and way marked, but in certain locations signposts and waymarks have a habit of going missing on a fairly regular basis. Granted, it is marked on the new Ordnance Survey Explorer map of the South Pennines, but reading that from the back of a horse on top of the moor in a high wind can sometimes be impossible. And the third reason is that people were simply getting lost. The South Pennines has a large number of bridleways, and at each junction there is often a choice of several different ways to go. A guidebook that you can slip into your pocket seemed the obvious answer.

People go wrong for two main reasons: either they are talking so much they fail to notice the signs, or they ask the locals how to get to the next B&B. The locals will certainly oblige and tell them the most direct way, but most likely it won't be the Pennine Bridleway. One group of horseriders managed to miss out half the Loop by asking the way to the next B&B and getting directed straight down the main road. So, if lost, do not ask the locals. Look at the book.

There are certain places where people go wrong on a regular basis. Take extra notice at the following places: Bottomley - see page 7 clockwise, and page 31 anticlockwise. Calderbrook - see page 9 clockwise, and page 30 anticlockwise. Healey Dell - see page 13 clockwise and page 25 anticlockwise. For these and other tricky bits, we have included thumbnail sketch maps to help you find where you should be going, and we have also included warnings in the text.

The guide was originally written for riders doing the Loop over three days to tell them how to get from one B&B to the next. For this book the 47-mile circular route has been split up into short sections of between 2 and 5 miles, mostly from one main road crossing to another. These distances should give you an idea of your riding speed – if you are taking 2 hours to complete a 4 mile section you are going to be out a long time if you hope to cover 18 miles in a day! Grid references have been put in at the beginning of these sections to help with map reading, and bold text has been used to help you spot the more prominent landmarks around the route to make the text easier to follow.

If you are riding the entire Loop the easiest place to start your ride is from a B&B that provides parking – please check as not all farms have the room for box parking, and most make a small charge. If you are not starting from a B&B there are a few car parks and quiet places that are suitable to unload horses or bikes (but not for overnight parking).

● Both clockwise and anticlockwise guides have started at the Long Causeway, Cliviger as Maiden's Cross car park opposite the wind farm GR 894 298 is a short distance from the Mary Towneley Loop and makes an ideal starting place.

● Other possible car parks are in the centre of Waterfoot, either off Ashworth Street GR 836 218, or behind the Co-op GR 833 217, and at Watergrove reservoir GR 912 176.

● There is also a very small car park at the side of the road near Widdop reservoir, but this is usually busy at weekends, and unless it is your nearest access point, travelling horses along this road is not recommended.

● Other quiet places are Catley Lane Head known as the Bottom of Rooley Moor, GR 869 161, or near Lobden Golf Course, GR 892 175.

The Pennine Bridleway is a bridleway, and first national trail specifically designated for horseriders. It is there for walkers and mountain–bikers as well, although the mountain–bikers must give way to riders and walkers. In certain sections it can also be used by motor vehicles: both motorbikes and 4-wheel drives.

It is there for everyone to enjoy, and that means treating other users with courtesy and respect. Horse riders are advised to check the 'News' section on the Natural England website www. nationaltrail.co.uk/penninebridleway for events held on the Loop such as the Mountain Bike Challenge usually held in May. This involves a high entry of approximately 300 bikers who ride the Loop in a day.

We recommend that you use this book along with the *Map and Services Guide to the Mary Towneley Loop,* published free by Natural England and updated on a regular basis. It contains all sorts of information including overnight stops, parking places, facilities and services such as farriers, vets and the location of pubs, and for the non-horseriders bus and railway links. It can be obtained from tourist information centres, from Natural England Publications (tel. 0870 120 6466) quoting the reference no. CA 29, or from the Pennine Bridleway team based in Manchester (tel. 0161 237 1061). Several public houses have been mentioned in the text, but if you are hoping for a pub lunch check their opening times as some of the rural ones are not open at lunchtime during the week.

All users are strongly advised to carry a South Pennines Land Ranger map Explorer 21, and suitable waterproof clothing as you are travelling some of the highest paths in the Pennines where the weather can change quickly and the temperature plummet.

Lastly, if riding have your horse shod before you leave home, as there is nothing more infuriating than having your ride cut short by a lost horse shoe.

Acknowledgements

The author would like to thank the following people for their assistance with the productions of this book:

Forest of Rossendale Bridleway Association, whose financial support made this book a reality.

Our advertisers, whose generous support has contributed to the printing costs of the book.

The Towneley Trail Riding Farm Group for their encouragement and hospitality during research.

Sue Hogg of the South Pennine Packhorse Trails Trust for her contributions to the text.

John B. Taylor for the maps and illustrations.

Frank Woolrych and the Hebden Bridge Literary and Scientific Society (Local History Section) for permission to reproduce the photograph of Horsehold.

Barry Greenwood for permission to use front and back cover photos of Lady Towneley.

Richard Peace of Excellent Books for photos of walkers and cyclists using the Loop.

Titus Thornber for the Limegals drawing.

Ordnance Survey.

Cosi Towneley for her contributions to the text.

And, last but not least, Wendy Taylor for making sense of it and putting the whole thing together.

Mary Towneley: The Begetter of the Pennine Bridleway

The idea of a national trail for horses along the spine of England came to my mother in the 1970s. By the 80s it had insinuated itself throughout the house, taking over many a room, wall and bookcase as the array of maps, books, photographs and articles grew to overwhelming proportions.

First and foremost, my mother was a wonderful storyteller. As children, she hauled us, not natural walkers, along Hadrian's Wall. Tired, with soggy feet, chilled hands and dripping noses, these factors were forgotten as she captivated us with tales of the lost Ninth Legion and ghostly encounters with Roman cavalry. Liberated from school, my youngest sister and I picnicked in the hollows of Badbury Rings or in the Iron Age hill forts perched on Hod or Ham, whilst listening to the last stand of some Celtic kingdom. Each geological feature or building visited had a history, fact or fiction, that my mother vividly brought to life. So it is unsurprising that the remains of lost and forgotten ancient highways, visible only to a few as they snake over the tops of our Pennine moorlands, should ignite her interest. The idea of linking all these empty ways became an intriguing dip into the annals of history, literature, folklore and fact. It placed the landscape she loved in a light seldom considered by those tramping these lonely ways, many of whom remain ignorant of the important role such routes played in putting the Great into Britain. From the pit to the pack – England's wealth was transported on the hoof.

Secondly, my mother was a 'doer'. Having produced and set on their way seven children, she continued to hunt twice a week, and when the season was over to prepare her beloved 14.2 hh chestnut mare, Miss Muffet, for the rigours of the then embryonic long-distance riding season. This required her to cover numerous miles a week and, not being one to stick to the same tracks until the monotony dulled the pleasure for rider and horse alike, she looked for and explored obscure and not-so-obscure links. What could not be ridden immediately was stored for another day until it became a standing joke that 'Anyone coming for a short ride?' meant anything up to four hard hours in the saddle. We continued to fall for it – her horizons kept unfolding.

In September 1986, following two years of research, four friends – Dawn Baly, Mary Cranfield, Jane Rowell and my mother - gathered near Corbridge, Northumberland. They had a combined age of over 220 years, and Mary Cranfield had just undergone a double hip replacement. Their aim - to ride by hook or crook to Parsley Hey in Derbyshire. They would use the lost and forgotten ways, abandoned with the onset of mechanized transport in the late nineteenth and early twentieth century. And so they embarked along the drove roads, black ways, corpse roads, limersgates, saltways and packhorse trails, following in the footsteps of Defoe, the intrepid Celia Fiennes, the dogged Lady Anne Clifford, the last packman Ailse o'Fussers and her donkey Jerry, and the strings of Galloway ponies that carried the packs that fuelled and sustained the voracious appetite of commerce throughout the length and breadth of Britain.

Dawn, Mary and my mother were the riders, while Jane, with her dog Dilly, took on the unenviable role of back-up. No mobile phones then, just a packet of flares which they never had to use, and I continue to carry to this day.

It took a mere nine days to cover the 250 odd miles over some of the wildest, wettest and most isolated terrain in the country. They were not out for a hack: this party meant business, averaging 27 miles a day. A precedent was set: it could be done. Now to negotiate the corridors of power.

To the politician the horse is one of two things: a sign of wealth to be condemned, or a sign of danger to be contained. In both cases to be ignored as undeserving of consideration.

The completion of this initial ride proved riders were no longer prepared to sit on the sidelines whilst others stole their heritage from them with wire, locks and tarmac. It also implied a steely determination to succeed even in the face of such ignorant comments as those written by one Minister, who thought that:

> 'Creating this new trail will do nothing for the rights of way target for the year 2000. The existing bridleways can be used but it is questionable whether there is any sense in joining them up.'

This view, considering there was and remains a regular statistical return of 3000 or so accidents per year involving horses on the road, leaves one breathless by its lack of vision or concern.

The history from this point is clearly documented. The Countryside Commission (subsequently the Countryside Agency) took the Pennine Bridleway project under its wing. Based in the Manchester office, its progress was masterminded by the team of Jim McQueen, and Sue Rogers. Sue's job was to identify the best route and work out all the details. She was inundated with suggestions and offers of assistance from the many bridleway groups and horseriders up and down the Pennines. Down in Saddleworth Edith Boon, chairman of the West Pennine BA, called a meeting to work out possible alternative routes leading north from Derbyshire. When it looked as though the whole project was about to stall, riders wrote letters to the Minister. Even so, it took six years for the proposal to receive official blessing.

In January 1995 John Gummer, as Secretary of State for the Environment, finally approved the submission. It is not the exact route taken by the original merry band, and, indeed, the northern route has yet to be finalized. The Mary Towneley Loop was opened in 2002, and the southern section from Littleborough to Hartington or Middleton Top, Derbyshire, in May 2004.

In buying this book I would urge you to consider joining your local bridleway group or supporting the South Pennine Packhorse Trails Trust. In East Lancashire/West Yorkshire border area Chris Peat for the Forest of Rossendale Bridleways Association (FoRBA) and Sue Hogg (SPPTT) worked closely with my mother. They epitomize the determination and selflessness found in all those who seek to protect our ancient highways and improve the bridleway network for horseriders and other members of the public to enjoy, both now and in the future. They sit on endless committees, write reams of letters and articles and suffer countless setbacks. Yet they stoically continue the battle against ignorance and prejudice on behalf of every rider who wants to follow the spirit of my mother over that next horizon.

As you ride the Loop, enchanted and amazed by the views which will open up for you at each peak and corner, salute them. They deserve our support for in the words of that memorable Arabic saying:

*'The wind of heaven is that
which blows between a horse's ears.'*

Cosima Towneley **February 2004**

Widdop Reservoir from Gorple Road

Cant Clough Reservoir

THE MARY TOWNELEY LOOP

BURNLEY

WORSTHORNE

HURSTWOOD

Townley Hall

Townley Arms

Daysledge

CLIVIGER

Rams

Cornside

Thieveley Pike

Holme Chpl

Lovesgate

Deerplay

WEIR

Holme Chpl

WATER

LUMB

Hargreaves Arms

Campbell's Cross

A682

Cambridge Res.

Castle Clough Res.

Coal Clough Wind Farm 24 turbines

The Long Causeway

Huntroyd Res.

Gorple Road

Widdop Res.

Gorple Res.

Reaps Cross

Cant Clough Res.

Standstone / bushings at Shedden

Monkroyd Hill

North Dean

New Delight

COLDEN

Pennine Way

HEPTONSTALL

Hardcastle Crags

A6033

Lumb Falls

Hebble Hole Clough

Colden Valley

HEBDEN BRIDGE

Mount Cross

Bridestones

EASTWOOD

SHORE

CORNHOLME

A646

Whirlaw

WHITELEES

TODMORDEN

Lower Rough Head

Roade

A646

Sportsman's

A671

Banana Footbridge

Packhorse

Mt. View hole

Backpack Res.

WALSDEN / FORD

M65

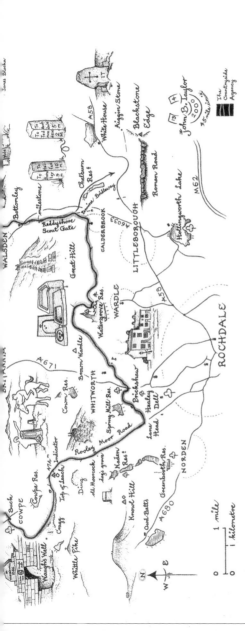

Presented by Her Royal Highness Princess Anne to Lady Mary Towneley on behalf of The Countryside Agency in recognition of Lady Mary Towneley's outstanding contribution to the development of the Pennine Bridleway

Path at Sheddon showing lime burning spoil heaps

Gorple Reservoir from the summit of Gorple Gate

The Mary Towneley Loop Clockwise

LONG CAUSEWAY, COALCLOUGH TO
HURSTWOOD RESERVOIR GR 891 291   2 MILES

At the end of the roadside track turn off to the left (north) onto Worsthorne Moor, leaving the wind farm behind you. This section of bridleway has 3 horsestiles on it. Ride down the first section of track, **Cant Clough Reservoir** is in the distance, and turn left at the T–junction. Cross over the stream and ride down between a series of strange humps both sides of the track – these are the spoil heaps from the lime burning industry which occupied Shedden several hundred years ago. The lime kilns where the lime was heated to separate it from the waste material are long gone and the spoil is all that remains.

Go down to the next stream crossing and turn left and ride along with the stream on your left to yet another stream crossing. After fifty yards you come to an old packhorse bridge over the stream. Turn right over the bridge and ride up the hill to **Cant Clough Reservoir** and ride across the dam head. At the far end after going through a gate, go up the hill on the concrete track, leaving Cant Clough behind, and make for **Hurstwood Reservoir.**

HURSTWOOD RESERVOIR TO
GORPLE LOWER RESERVOIR GR 889 315   5 MILES

Take the track running along the banks of the reservoir and ride up to meet Gorple Road, turning right. From here it is 2 miles to **Widdop Reservoir** along a well-defined bridleway known as Gorple Gate or Limersgate. Once on Gorple Road, do not leave the hard track as there are deep bogs to the sides. At the summit you cross the border from Lancashire into Yorkshire then it is a short distance to **Halifax Road.** Turn right and ride ³/₄ mile down the road to where the PB turns off to the right (south) through a gate and horsestile. Follow the water board road all the way up to **Gorple Lower Reservoir.**

GORPLE LOWER RESERVOIR TO BADGER LANE, BLACKSHAW HEAD GR 944 317   5 MILES

Ride over the dam head and turn left, passing the water board house on the left. Just after the house turn right through a green wrought iron gate onto a stony track that climbs up the hill for $1/2$ mile. At the top of the hill pass through a gate onto a farm road, **Edge Lane,** which soon turns to tarmac. Ride for a mile along this lane and after a property on the left called **Longtail** take the first tarmac lane (slippery) on the right heading down the steep hill to the house in the bottom surrounded by trees, passing **School Lane Farm** and **The Barn** on the left. (If you carry on a short distance further along Edge Lane there is a farm shop called May's that serves sandwiches, homemade pies, drinks and sells thirteen different types of champagne.)

Ride over the bridge and admire the gardens of Land Farm on the left: these are open to the public in the summer months. The bridleway, known as Sunderland Lane, is part of a medieval road that crossed the Calder valley to Erringden, a deer park belonging to the Manor of Wakefield in former times.

The path skirts around the back of the house and narrows up the hill to a bridleway gate. The track runs uphill through a deep holloway and there is a small water trough off to the right at the top. Pass through several more gates until the PB crosses a farm access road, New Road. Go straight across onto a walled lane, this section of track has a property on the left – Field Head Farm - surrounded by sycamore trees, with two ponds on the left below the track. Go through the gate in front of you into the field and follow the next section of bridleway for $1/2$ mile until you come to the property at the top of **Brown Hill Lane.**

Turn left on Brown Hill Lane and ride down to meet the main road. At the road turn left and ride 500 yards down the hill to the sharp left hand bend (the New Delight public house is on the left below the bend). Take the lane off to the right and ride along to the first house on the right, Shaw Bottom House and turn right, following the PB up the hill on a narrow walled lane, Bow Lane, and down the other side to meet **Badger Lane.** (To reach Badger Fields Farm B&B turn left on Badger Lane and ride for approximately 400 yards down Badger Lane to find the farm on the left.)

BADGER LANE, BLACKSHAW HEAD TO A646 TODMORDEN–HEBDEN BRIDGE ROAD GR 964 275 2 MILES

On reaching Badger Lane turn left and take the first bridleway on the right, Marsh Lane, which is also a farm access road. Ignore the first track off to the right to a farm and the next bridleway off to the left, and carry on down the hill. At the bottom of the track at the gate into **Dove Scout Farm,** turn left on the narrow packhorse trail which descends steeply down the hill. Stoodley Pike is directly in front of you on the skyline – you will be riding along the foot of the hill below the pike later in the day

Follow the path down the hill, round to the right, sharp left, then sharp right into the woods until you come to a **T–junction.** Turn right and follow the track down the hill, sharp left with the waterfalls and stream on your right – this is Jumble Hole Clough. Lower down you pass between some cottages and detached houses until you pass under the railway bridge before meeting the A646 Hebden Bridge–Todmorden road, with the **C V S builders' yard** on the right. Take the fenced **bridleway to the left that runs parallel** to the road and follow it along to the end and then between some lock up garages. Turn right to the **Pegasus crossing.**

A646 TODMORDEN–HEBDEN BRIDGE ROAD TO
MANKINHOLES GR 971 264   4¹/₂ MILES

Cross the main road on to Callis Wood Bottom, over the river and take the track straight ahead over the canal bridge. Follow the stony track up the hill through the trees passing through a gate next to a cattle grid. The track turns sharp right, and then sharp left in front of a house, carry on up the hill, and take the left fork following the PB signs. Follow the track round until it meets the main farm access road again and turn left up the hill. Just before the top of the hill where the track bends slightly right the Pennine Bridleway **(PB)** follows the narrow path off to the left dropping steeply down to the **packhorse bridge over the stream**. After closing the gate the PB turns right (for the hamlet of Horsehold carry straight on along the edge of the wood and turn right on reaching the farm road).

The PB follows the new path up the hill and through a gate, then on to a second gate. Turn right here onto a grassed track (Pinnacle Lane) with Stoodley Pike in front of you. The track turns sharp left onto a gravel track and leads up to the cross roads - turn right on to Kilnshaw Lane. Kilnshaw Lane runs into London Road and passes along the base of the hill on Langfield Common under **Stoodley Pike,** bringing you into the village of **Mankinholes**.

The stone obelisk on top of Stoodley Pike is the second monument to be built there. The first was put up in 1814 to mark end of the Napoleonic wars, but fell down in 1854 at the outbreak of the Crimean War. A second (the present) monument was built in 1856, with some financial assistance from the Freemasons.

Kilnshaw Lane

Snoodle Hill from Reddyshore Scout

Rooley Moor Road showing the section cobbled during the cotton famine of 1850/60

Cowpe Reservoir

MANKINHOLES TO A6033 LITTLEBOROUGH–
TODMORDEN ROAD, BOTTOMLEY GR 961 234　　3 MILES

Turn right (there is a set of water troughs on the right here) and ride through the village; take the first bridleway off to the left opposite a converted Methodist Sunday School called Lane Head. (To reach Cross Farm B&B carry on along the tarmac highway.) Follow this causewayed track down to the **Top Brink** public house (note the milestone at the bottom) and go straight across onto a very narrow stone–sett packhorse track which descends steeply for 100 yards before abruptly terminating on a tarmac road in Lumbutts village. Turn right and ride for about 1 mile up the road.

> Mankinholes is a very early settlement, but most of the stone buildings date from the 18th century, and have fine mullioned windows with drip courses. The prosperity of the yeoman farmers was based on the dual economy of agriculture and cloth. Wool (much of which was imported from other parts of the country) was spun and woven at home, and the outline of the 'takking in' doors can still be seen on some of the house walls. This door gave access up a flight of stone steps from the road direct to the upper storey where the weaving was done.

> By contrast, Lumbutts is an early industrial village in character, and once boasted a school and a Co-op, which only closed in the 1960s. The village grew to provide the workforce for the four cotton mills powered by the stream in Lumbutts Clough. The square tower by the activities centre is all that remains of Lumbutts mill, which was built in the 1790s.

Just before the **Shepherd's Rest** public house on the right the PB forks left through a gate onto Langfield Common to pick up another old packhorse track known as **Salter Rake Gate**. This was once the main road to Rochdale, Manchester and Cheshire and is a good example of a traditional stone causeway. It crosses a farm track and then runs into a walled section (another milestone known as the Shurcrack Guide is on the left), and then continues across open moor for nearly 1 mile as it climbs gently around the shoulder of the hill (Rake End) until you come into the small hamlet known as **Hollingworth.** (See map.)

The first house on the left has a **red telephone box** in the garden – ride along the tarmac lane as it bends round to the left passing North Hollingworth Farm on the right. Do not turn right here unless you wish to ride $1/2$ mile down the steep tarmac lane to some shops on the main road at Walsden. (Highlands on the left does B&B for horses and riders.)

Continue on the tarmac lane for ¹/₄ mile past several detached houses until the last white cottage on the left. Pass through the gate near the house and keep to the stone causeway packhorse route that follows the wall through a narrow gate. After this gate the path drops down sharply to a white house on the right called **Dean Royd Farm.** (See map.)

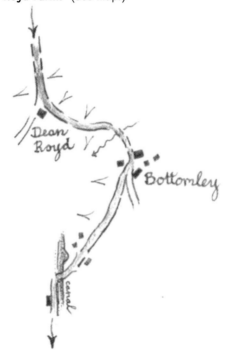

Dean Royd & Bottomley

As you ride down this section of hillside look ahead and you can see the route you will take down to the main road and up the steep hillside onto Reddyshore Scout. Follow the path along the shoulder of the hill riding above Dean Royd Farm, and continue down to a gated **bridge** over Black Clough and ride up between two buildings into the hamlet of **Bottomley.** Turn right and immediately fork right through a gate onto the packhorse route which drops steeply down the hill to cross the canal before reaching a tarmac lane. Follow the lane between the cottages up to the **main Littleborough–Todmorden road, A6033.**

A6033 LITTLEBOROUGH-TODMORDEN ROAD TO WATERGROVE RESERVOIR
GR 941 208   4 ¹/₂ **MILES**

Turn left at the main road (see map) using the grass verge and ride along for about 100 yards to the **Pegasus crossing.**

Cross the main road and ride up the field edge to a gate. Turn left onto a grass track and go through two gates.

Once through the gates the path starts to climb steeply up the hill and zigzags to ease the gradient – look out for the marker posts –

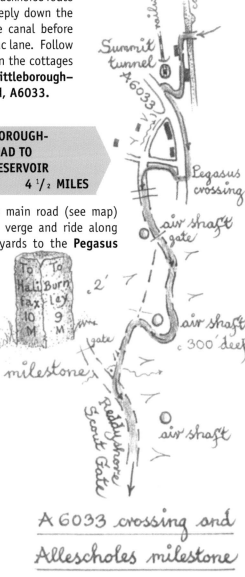

A 6033 crossing and Allescholes milestone

8

until you eventually reach the top, known as **Reddyshore Scout**. There is an old guidestoop (the Allescholes milestone) on the right at the top to confirm you are on an old packhorse route. The climb to the top is 450 feet.

If you suffer from vertigo, now is the time to dismount or get out the blindfold! Turn left on the track and ride past **two pylons** with a **bridge** between, until this access road drops down to meet **Calderbrook Road**. (See map.) **Ignore the sign off to the left – Pennine Bridleway Chelburn – as this is the southern section of the PB which takes you down to Derbyshire.** The Mary Towneley Loop carries on along the level tarmac road for

about 100 yards. The Todmorden–Rochdale railway line is buried deep in the hillside at this point, and on the right are two large round towers – these are the ventilation shafts for the railway line. After the **airshafts** take the tarmac farm road that forks off to the right and immediately look for the sign indicating the PB going straight ahead as the farm road swings right. Follow this narrow grass bridleway along until you come onto a tarmac lane between several detached houses, and follow the lane along until you leave the houses behind. After going round a couple of sharp bends you come to

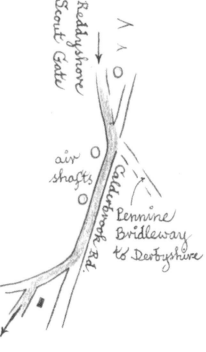

some **cottages on both sides** of the road, being known as **Calderbrook**, and as the road starts to descend look for the PB turning right in front of **Calderbrook House** with its wrought iron gates. (From here to Watergrove Reservoir is about 3 miles.) Follow the track up past the Pennine Trout Fisheries, on the left, teeming with 10lb+ trout, and continue along to the first farm which is an Arab stud. Once through the gate by this farm take the left hand track at the fork, and follow this new section of track for 2^1/$_2$ miles. The path crosses a stream via a beautiful new ford, and goes through several gates. You will pass two bridleways off to the left – also notice to the left the view of Hollingworth Lake and the Rakewood Viaduct of the M62 some 3 miles away as the crow flies. Go through another gate in the wall and as you come round the hill you will see **Watergrove Reservoir** below you. As you ride down towards the reservoir you pass the Tree for Life Memorial Forest on your left.

> *The catchment area around Watergrove Reservoir was once a thriving farming community and there were 46 farms or cottages in the valley, the oldest dating from 1509. The village of Watergrove to the south side of the reservoir consisted of a church, 40 houses, 2 pubs – the Orchard and the Trap Inn, 4 mills and a smithy. The village was demolished and the site is now covered by the reservoir. All that remains to be seen during times of drought is Ramsden Road, which continued in a southerly direction from the drinking trough at the warden's office. The valley is formed by 4 hills, Brown Wardle and Middle Hill to the west, Hades and Rough Hill to the north. Rough Hill at 1425 feet above sea level is the highest, but the most spectacular views are from the top of Brown Wardle at 1314 feet above sea level. Mesolithic (early Stoneage) flint and Neolithic (late Stoneage) stone axes, along with a Bronze Age barrow have been found on Hades Hill.*

WATERGROVE TO A671 (ROCHDALE-BACUP ROAD), BROADLEY GR 912 181   4 MILES

On reaching the main track near the reservoir, turn right. (To reach Half Way House B&B turn left at this point.) When you reach the warden's office (toilets here) and visitor centre on the left, follow the setted track to the right (see map), where you will see a horse trough. Ride up this road through a gate and soon after the track becomes stony take the left fork and ride down to **Higher Slack Brook Nature Reserve**.

Take the **bridge** over the stream and go through the gate in the fence line in front of you and turn right on the track. Follow it along past **two ponds** on the right, and then left into a notch between the hills. This narrow paved path soon opens out onto the moor, and becomes little more than a sheep track. Keep going straight ahead and up with the large hill known as Brown Wardle directly in front of you until you come to the first main track where you turn left. There is a post with a blue bridleway

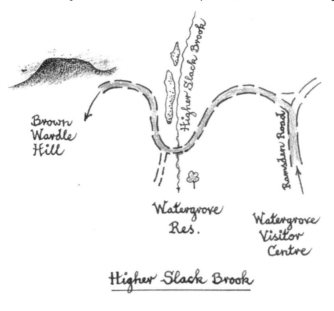

Brown Wardle Hill

Higher Slack Brook

Ramsden Road

Watergrove Res.

Watergrove Visitor Centre

Higher Slack Brook

sign here. This track is for the most part black cinders – follow it along until it splits and take the left fork, still a cinder path running parallel to a wider stone track. At the junction continue straight ahead riding towards **Lobden Golf Clubhouse.** The track goes through a couple of bends, then passes up the **left hand side** of the clubhouse. At the next fork after the clubhouse go left and follow a stony track past a **cream farmhouse,** then a **white farmhouse**, both on the right. (See map.)

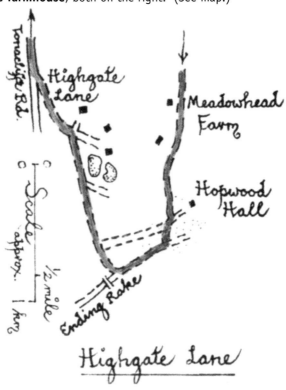

Follow the track with a third house, Hopwood Hall, off to the left, with a **church spire** in front of you. Cross the access track to Hopwood Hall onto a short new section of bridleway until you meet an old stony bridleway. Turn right with a stone wall on your left and ride along to a gate. Go through the gate and ignore the first track immediately on the right, but continue along 50 yards, turning right before the stone bridge. Having turned right follow the track as it skirts the spoil heaps and disused quarries now full of water. At the end the path meets a tarmac lane – Highgate Lane. Continue on the PB turn left and ride down the hill. At the T–junction turn right onto **Tonacliffe Road**. At the next junction turn left onto **Oakenshaw Avenue**. This short road takes you down to the main A671 Rochdale–Bacup road, Market Street. (See map.)

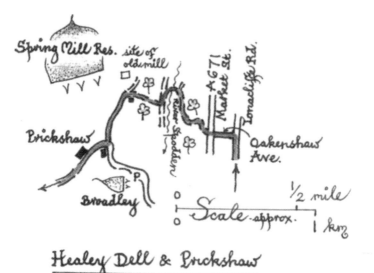

Healey Dell & Prickshaw

A671 ROCHDALE–BACUP ROAD, BROADLEY TO
TOP OF LEACH GR 882 168   4 MILES.

Go straight across the main road onto the PB, which goes downhill
and sweeps to the left to meet the River Spodden. Ride along
with the river on your left for 300 yards to the bridge, cross over
and turn back with the river on your left again. Take the first
track on the right and follow it up through the trees ignoring a
small track off to the right. The bridleway is joined by another
path from the left and goes up the hill with a stream on the
left. Ride between the wooden posts to meet a track and turn
left. Continue along the track through the remains of **Spring
Mill**, now derelict and follow **Prickshaw Lane** up the hill to the
hamlet of **Broadley Fold**.

Take the track to the right, **Knacks Lane,** and follow it until it
goes downhill, past a house on the bend known as **The Waste**,
and continue up to the **cattle grid**. Once through the gate, take
the middle of three lanes bearing slightly to the right. Ride along
for $1/4$ mile to the crossroads and turn right passing through a
metal barrier onto a wide road. This is **Rooley Moor Road**.

> *Rooley Moor Road is a very old highway linking Rossendale
> and Burnley to Rochdale. However, you will notice that a
> stretch of it is setted – this was done during the cotton
> famine of the 1850's and 1860's when there was no work
> for the poor of Rossendale and the township employed them
> to pave the road. Nearer to the Cowpe end the track is
> paved with a double row of stone slabs which have grooves
> worn into them – this is part of the route used by the
> quarrymen to take stone out of the quarries, the main one
> being Cragg quarry.*

After two miles the track forks; keep to the right, and after another
mile the track forks again – keep to the left on the level paved
road – the right fork is the continuation of Rooley Moor Road
and it starts to bear down the hill to Stacksteads. Near to this
junction up on the hill on your left is a large stone known as Top

of Leach, which marks the boundary between the former districts of Whitworth, Bacup, Haslingden and Rawtenstall before they were amalgamated into the Borough of Rossendale. This is the highest point on the loop at 474 metres above sea level.

TOP OF LEACH TO A681 WATERFOOT GR 851 197
3¹/₂ MILES

You are on the remains of the old tramway at this point, and as you progress a splendid view opens out on your right of **Cowpe Reservoir** with Waterfoot and Bacup in the valley below. After riding for some distance between the hills the track opens out again and on your left is the wide-open space of Scout Moor, an Urban Common, upon which local farmers have grazing rights. During the summer months you may encounter loose horses. In the distance beyond Scout Moor is Holcombe Tower perched on the end of Holcombe Hill. Soon the track bends to the left and then the right with a fence line on your right. At the end of the fence you will see a wooden gate in front of you taking you off the moor.

As you ride down the hill the Rossendale Valley stretches to the left and right as far as you can see. To the left is Cloughfold, Waterfoot is below you and Bacup is to the right. As you get lower down the hill Cowpe Reservoir comes into view again.

Follow the track down the field until it brings you onto the concrete access road to **Tippet Farm B&B.** Continue on down the steep hill to Cowpe, turning right then left at the bottom to join the highway, Cowpe Road. The Buck Inn is on your right at this point. Turn left and ride down Cowpe Road taking care on the bends, then turn right onto **Lumb Holes Lane**. On the bend turn left onto **Bridge Street**, and then left at the end onto **Carr Lane.** Ride down the hill and re-join Cowpe Road; continuing past **Waterfoot Health Centre**. (To reach Dam Top Riding Centre turn left and ride along the river.) To continue on the PB, before you meet Bacup Road, A681, turn right along the river with the coal yard on your left. At the end turn left to the Pegasus Crossing on Bacup Road.

A681 RAWTENSTALL–BACUP ROAD, WATERFOOT TO
B6238 BURNLEY ROAD EAST, LUMB GR 836 217   3¹/₂ MILES

From the Pegasus crossing ride up Townsend Street, which runs into Millar Barn Lane, past the **Grammar School** to the junction with Booth Road and turn left down the hill. Take the first street on the right – **Todd Carr Road** with the B&E Boys business on the corner. Ride to the end of the street and take the path on your right up the edge of **Edgeside Park**. At the top of the park the path drops you onto the road again – carry on uphill and take the rough tarmac road to the left. This brings you out onto **Edgeside Lane**. Turn left and ride all the way along to the crossroads at the end and go straight across onto Lumb Lane. After passing between several properties the lane becomes bridleway and after a mile brings you down to **Burnley Road East B6238.**

B6238 BURNLEY ROAD EAST, LUMB TO
A671 BACUP ROAD, DEERPLAY GR 838 250   3 MILES

(Note – this section has numerous gates, all of which are horse friendly.) Turn right and after 50 yards take **Peers Clough Road** on the left. Ride up Peers Clough Road passing several farms – (Peers Clough Farm B&B is ¹/₂ mile up the hill on the left) – until the last farm at the top. The bridleway continues through a gate up the hill to a junction with five gates. Take the last gate on the right and ride down the field edge. Go through two more single gates to a pair of gates where the bridleway crosses a farm road, and follow the PB down the field edge with a hedge on your right. Go down the hill, over a stream, turn left and continue up crossing two farm access roads riding towards a gate by a tree. Carry on up the hill crossing a third farm road until you see a PB sign pointing to the right. Ride down this section of track with a wall on your right and at the end turn right and ride down to **Burnley Road East B6238**. Cross the road at the red tarmac crossing and follow the bridleway to the left parallel to the road. At the top follow it round to the right, along and then to the left to the **Bacup Road A671** crossing.

A671 BACUP–BURNLEY ROAD, DEERPLAY TO
LONG CAUSEWAY, COALCLOUGH GR 857 274   3 MILES

Go across the road, again on a red tarmac strip and turn left riding
parallel to the road. Go through the gate in front of you and
continue along the track to the end. Where you see the cattle
grid on the left there are two tracks off to the right – take the
second one signed PB Holme Chapel. After $1/2$ mile follow the PB
sign off to the left avoiding Cow Side Farm, rejoining the rough
farm track beyond the farm.

Continue along and where the farm road turns sharp left go
through the gate in front of you into the field. In the corner of
the field is the stone in memory of Mary. As the stone suggests,
pause a while and survey the magnificent views before riding
down the steep hill aptly named Heartbreak Hill by Mary. At the
bottom of the hill, in the hamlet of Stonehouses, follow the track
round to the right between some ruined farm buildings, and along
passing **Scout Farm**. On joining Scout Farm access road, do not
follow it under the railway line, but ride along with the railway
line on your left to pass under the second bridge and to the main
A646 Burnley–Todmorden Road in Holme Chapel.

At the A646 the **Ram Inn** is on your right – horses are welcome
to use the paddock whilst you have a swift drink or lunch. Follow
the PB up the lane opposite the Ram, forking right at the top
onto Holme Chapel Road, an ancient highway, now a green lane.
The PB forks off to the right after $1/4$ mile, through a new gate
in the fenceline. After 100 yards turn right to avoid the farm.
Follow the track downhill to a gate on the left, then up the hill
to turn right through another gate. The track then runs parallel
to the **Long Causeway** to the **second gate**. Cross the Long
Causeway at the red tarmac strip and take the new path running
alongside the road.

Towneley Trail Bed & Box

Excellent accommodation situated directly on the Mary Towneley Loop with panoramic views across the surrounding countryside.

Highlands is a detached home with five acres and stabling for equestrian purposes. Unlimited riding available with access to miles of bridleways.

Double, Twin or Single Rooms
Private Bathroom & Shower Room
Two reception rooms
Dining Room
Large Kitchen
Snooker Room with full size table
Outdoor Heated Swimming Pool
Summer House with showering/wc facilities
Private Parking

HORSE AND RIDER PACKAGE
Evening Meal,
Bed & Full English Breakfast.
Stabling/grazing+hard feed,
Packed lunch
Non riding packages
also available

Mrs Sue Wright, Highlands, Hollingworth Lane, Walsden,
Todmorden, Lancashire. OL14 6QY
Tel: 01706 817432 Mobile 07775 598221 Fax 01706 818835.
Email sue@towneleytrailbedandbox.co.uk

Some of the contributors to Mary's Stone

The unveiling of Mary's Stone by Sir Simon Towneley

The Mary Towneley Loop Anticlockwise

LONG CAUSEWAY, COALCLOUGH TO A671 BACUP–BURNLEY ROAD, DEERPLAY GR 891 291   **3 MILES**

At the Long Causeway turn right or west and ride along the path at the roadside leaving the windfarm behind. At the red tarmac strip cross the road into the field and ride along parallel to the Long Causeway, and turn left after a gate, and ride down the hill. Follow the track that skirts Merrill Head Farm all the way until you come to Holme Chapel Road – an ancient highway now a green lane. Turn left onto Holme Chapel Road which takes you down to the A646 in the village of Holme Chapel. Opposite is the **Ram Inn** where horses are welcome to use the paddock at the back whilst you get a swift drink. The route turns right on the main road and immediately left down the side of the Ram.

At the end of this track turn right and ride along with the railway line on your left to the first underpass. Go under the line and turn right again to ride along the line. Follow the track through a gate and over a field until you meet the access road to Scout Farm. Ride along towards the farm a short distance and turn right through a bridlegate in the field fence, and take the new track across the field. This track avoids the yard and skirts the front of the house.

Ride past the house and at the fork keep left. Ride along this track for $1/_4$ mile until, just after the ruined farm buildings, you come to the hamlet of Stonehouses. Turn left up Mary's infamous "Heartbreak Hill", aptly named. At the top of this hill is the stone in memory of Mary. As the stone suggests, pause a while and survey the magnificent views. From Mary's stone exit the field onto the farm road and ride in a westerly direction slightly up hill. Follow the farm road for $1/_2$ mile or so until you see a new section of bridleway leading off to the right, which avoids riding through Cow Side Farm. The new section of track re-joins the farm road and follows it up to the A671 Bacup–Burnley road.

A671 BACUP ROAD, DEERPLAY TO B6238 WATERFOOT–BURNLEY ROAD, LUMB GR 857 274   3 MILES

Before you reach the A671, Bacup Road, turn left and ride the bridleway running parallel to the main road, passing through a gate, to the Bacup Road crossing. Cross the road and follow the track, which runs parallel to Bacup Road then Burnley Road East to the next road crossing. Cross the road and take the second track on the left and ride for $1/2$ mile to a T-junction. Turn left and follow the bridleway for $1/2$ mile crossing three farm roads, then bear right over a stream.

The next section has numerous gates all of which are horse friendly. Follow the field edge and at the top of the hill you meet yet another farm road. Turn left through the gate on the farm road and immediately take the bridleway to your right in the field, keeping to the field edge with the wall on your left. Follow this section along and then up a hill and, at the top, go through a gate and turn left. Ride down the hill past the farm on your left and join Peers Clough Road, a farm access road. (B&B is available at Peers Clough Farm – the first property on the right.) Ride down the hill all the way to meet the B6238, Burnley Road East.

B6238 BURNLEY ROAD EAST, LUMB TO A681 RAWTENSTALL–BACUP ROAD, WATERFOOT GR 838 250 $3^1/2$ MILES

At the junction of Peers Clough Road and the B6238 turn right onto Burnley Road East and immediately left onto the PB. Once on the cinder track keep to the right ignoring a private access road off to the left. This is Pinch Clough Road, which runs into Lumb Lane, and after nearly a mile brings you out at the junction with Shawclough Road and **Edgeside Lane**, both metalled roads. Go straight across onto Edgeside Lane and ride along until you see a lane off to the right down the side of a cottage, opposite

bungalow no. 246. Take care as you leave the highway – the tarmac is very smooth and steep for a few yards.

At the bottom take the new bridleway that runs along the edge of Edgeside Park. Follow this track down the hill to a junction of streets. Turn left onto **Todd Carr Road** with the Kingdom Hall Jehovah Witnesses building on the left and ride along to the T-junction at the end. Turn left onto Booth Road and ride up the hill, turning first right onto Millar Barn Lane down the side of the **Jolly Sailor** pub. Ride down the hill past the **Grammar School** to the junction with the A681, Bacup Road, where you will see a Pegasus crossing to the left.

A681 WATERFOOT TO TOP OF LEACH GR 836 217

3¹/₂ MILES

Using the crossing go across Bacup Road and ride around the back of the coal yard with the river on your left. (To reach Dam Top Riding Centre go straight across Cowpe Road.) To follow the PB, at the end turn left up Cowpe Road past **Waterfoot Health Centre** and after 20 yards take the left fork, Carr Lane. Ride up Carr Lane a short distance then turn right onto Bridge Street. At the end of Bridge Street turn right onto Lumb Holes Lane and re-join Cowpe Road. Go up the hill and just before the Buck Inn turn right and ride in front of a row of cottages called **Brooklands Terrace**. (See map.)

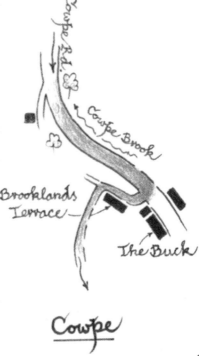

At the end of the terrace turn left onto the access road to **Tippet Farm**, where B&B is available. As the track swings around to the right the PB goes through a gate on the left into a field. Follow the PB up the steep hill; farther up the gradient slackens and the bridleway bears right around the shoulder of the hill and eventually up to a gate onto Scout Moor. This is urban common, upon which local farmers have grazing rights, so during the summer months you may encounter loose horses.

At the top stop for a breather as you have climbed approximately 700 feet. Follow the track, an old tramway, for a mile until you meet Rooley Moor Road.

> *Rooley Moor Road is a very old highway linking Rossendale and Burnley to Rochdale. However, you will notice that a stretch of it is setted – this was done during the cotton famine of the 1850's and 1860's when there was no work for the poor of Rossendale and the township employed them to pave the road. Nearer to the Cowpe end the track is paved with a double row of stone slabs which have grooves worn into them – this is part of the route used by the quarrymen to take stone out of the quarries, the main one being Cragg quarry.*

TOP OF LEACH TO A671 ROCHDALE–BACUP ROAD, BROADLEY GR 851 197   4 MILES

On the hill on your right is a large stone and trig point known as Top of Leach – the stone marks the boundary between the former districts of Whitworth, Bacup, Haslingden and Rawtenstall before they were amalgamated into the Borough of Rossendale. This is the highest point on the loop at 474m above sea level. You now have approximately 3 miles to cover on Rooley Moor Road before reaching Catley Lane Head, known as the "Bottom of Rooley Moor".

Halfway along Rooley Moor Road look over to the left – on the top of the line of hills you can see Stoodley Pike. You will ride underneath this on your way to Blackshaw Head. To the left at

10 o'clock the M62 snakes over the hill to Leeds, marked by the arches of Rakewood viaduct, with Hollingworth Lake below. In front of you are Rochdale and Manchester, and on a clear day Jodrell Bank near Knutsford in Cheshire is clearly visible.

Follow Rooley Moor Road all the way across the moor until it starts to descend. You will come to a cross roads after a metal barrier, and the PB takes the tarmac lane to the left. Ignoring a track off to the left, ride towards the cluster of cottages. Pass left in front of the cottages to the gate by a cattle grid. Follow the lane down the hill, past a property called **The Waste** and along to Broadley Fold. At the T-junction turn left (see map).

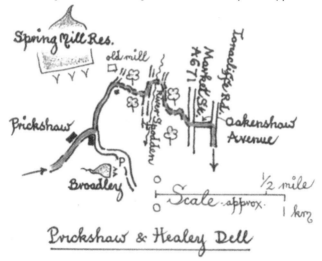

Prickshaw & Healey Dell

The lane at this point becomes very rough where the cobbles have lifted. Ride past the water board land on the left and a derelict mill, part of Spring Mill. **Twenty yards beyond the mill, as the lane turns to the left, take the track between the wooden posts.** The path goes down the hill through the trees, following the left fork to a T-junction. Turn left and ride alongside the River Spodden to the bridge. Go over the river and turn right riding along the path with the river now on your right. Follow the path up to the main Bacup–Rochdale road, the A671, Market Street.

A671 (ROCHDALE-BACUP ROAD) BROADLEY TO
WATERGROVE RESERVOIR GR 882 168   4 MILES

Go straight across onto Oakenshaw Avenue. At the T-junction
turn right onto Tonacliffe Road and, after **bungalow number 78**,
turn left onto Highgate Lane (see map). Follow the lane up the
hill for 200 yards. The bridleway takes the narrow path on the
right opposite the entrance to Highgate Farm.

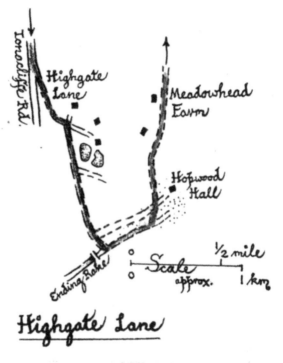

Follow this narrow grassy path, which skirts some disused quarries,
all the way down with the wall on your right. At the bottom you
meet a stone-sett road. Turn left and go through the gate in front
of you with a wall on your right. Follow the track for 50 yards until
you see a new track leading off to the left. Follow this across the
private access road to the house situated on the right (Hopwood

Hall) and head for the **white house** at the top of the hill. Carry on past a **cream farmhouse**, and head for another white building in the distance, which is **Lobden Golf Clubhouse**.

Take extra care on the next section to follow the PB signs as there are so many paths to choose from (see map). Follow the stone track with the clubhouse on your left to a junction of tracks. Turn right and ride under the power lines, passing the lane to **Tab Road Farm** on the right. After 20 yards turn left between the notch in the hillocks and **immediately** turn right. At the next junction take the path that forks off to the right and goes parallel to the main track. At this point you have the large hill known as Brown Wardle on your left.

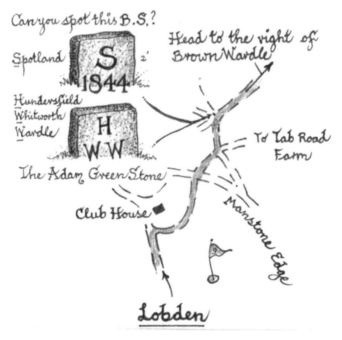

Can you spot this B.S.?

Spotland

S
1844 2'

Head to the right of
Brown Wardle

Hundersfield
Whitworth
Wardle

H
WW

To Tab Road
Farm

The Adam Green Stone

Club House

Manstone Edge

Lobden

At the end of this path you meet a **black cinder track**; follow it along the shoulder of the hill. After about $^1/_2$ mile the path turns right between **four trees** and heads down towards Watergrove

Reservoir. The PB fingerposts have now changed to smaller posts with a blue bridleway sign. Follow the track around to the right between two stone gateposts and onto a grassy section (see map). After 50 yards look for a faint path off to the right. Follow this path down the hill, then onto a steeper setted section in a **notch between two small hills**. At the bottom turn right and follow the track past two ponds to the gate on the left. This area is known as Higher Slack Brook Nature Reserve. Go through the gate and over the **bridge**, continuing up the hill to a gate near the top. At the top of the hill at the junction turn right and follow this track all the way down, onto a setted road, which runs down through a gate to the warden's office at Watergrove Reservoir. There is a horse trough on the left and, for the rider, the toilets are usually open.

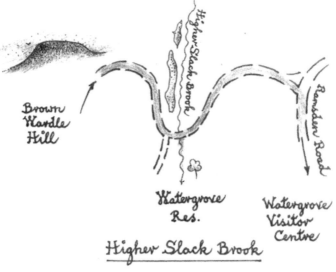

The catchment area around Watergrove Reservoir was once a thriving farming community and there were 46 farms or cottages in the valley, the oldest dating from 1509. The village of Watergrove to the south side of the reservoir consisted of a church, 40 houses, 2 pubs – the Orchard and the Trap Inn, 4 mills and a smithy. The village was

Drinking troughs at Mankinholes

Cyclists on Rooley Moor Road

Walkers on Rooley Moor Road

The air of heaven is that which blows between
a horse's ears

Lady Towneley M.B.E. 23.2.1935-13.2.2001
Pause awhile beside this monument and
remember Mary whose vision opened up
once more these ancient routes so that
you too can refresh your spirit as the
wild and romantic terrain of the
Pennine Bridleway unfolds before you.

Mary's Stone

Watergrove Reservoir in the drought showing Ramsden Road

demolished and the site is now covered by the reservoir. All that remains to be seen during times of drought is Ramsden Road, which continued in a southerly direction from the drinking trough at the warden's office. The valley is formed by 4 hills, Brown Wardle and Middle Hill to the west, Hades and Rough Hill to the north. Rough Hill at 1425 feet above sea level is the highest, but the most spectacular views are from the top of Brown Wardle at 1314 feet above sea level. Mesolithic (early Stoneage) flint and Neolithic (late Stoneage) stone axes, along with a Bronze Age barrow have been found on Hades Hill.

WATERGROVE TO A6033 LITTLEBOROUGH–TODMORDEN ROAD GR 912 181   4¹/₂ MILES

Turn left in front of the building. The track soon bends right round the side of the reservoir and after 50 yards take the left turn leading away from the reservoir and up the hill past the Tree for Life Memorial Forest. (To reach Half Way House B&B do not turn left but carry on down the track to Wardle.) To continue up the PB go up the stone-sett road and through the gate. Follow the track around the hill to the next wooden gate and turn right passing a bridleway on the right signed Shore after about ³/₄ mile.

Carry on over the stream crossing via a beautiful new ford, up to the next gate, and after several hundred yards you pass a farm on the right where they breed Arabs.

You are now dropping down towards Summit and you pass the Pennine Trout Fisheries on the right, teeming with 10lb+ trout, with a **church steeple** in front of you. On reaching the tarmac lane turn left and ride up past the cottages in Calderbrook. Follow the tarmac lane round a left bend then take the right fork and pass between several large houses. The tarmac soon turns to a narrow grass track which runs for about 300 yards, then ends at a tarmac farm road. Turn right and go down the hill to meet Calderbrook Road, disused at present.

The Todmorden–Rochdale railway line is buried deep in the hillside at this point (it is actually below the level of the canal), and on the left are two large round towers – these are the ventilation shafts for the railway line. **At the second air shaft you will see a sign on the right for the PB to Chelburn – this is the southern section of the PB leading to Derbyshire, and should be ignored.** The Mary Towneley Loop proceeds up the hill to a track forking off to the left. Follow this up and at a cattle grid take the right fork.

This brings you up onto Reddyshore Scout, and for the next few miles you will be following the ancient highway that was once the main road between Rochdale and Halifax.

If you suffer from vertigo, now is the time to dismount or get out the blindfold! Go through two gates with a pylon between, then after **100 yards,** **before the power lines,** (see map) take a narrow

railway

canal

Summit tunnel *A6033*

Pegasus crossing

air shaft *gate*

To Tod Mor dEN 2 M / To Roch dale 5 M — *milestone* — *c2'*

gate

air shaft *c300' deep*

Reddyshore Scout Gate

air shaft

Allescholes milestone and A6033 crossing

paved path off to the right which descends sharply down the hill. Note the old milestone (the Allescholes milestone) on your left as you turn. The path zigzags several times to ease the gradient.

At the bottom of the hill the PB passes through two gates then meets a farm road. Take the field on your right to the Pegasus crossing. Once across the main road turn left and ride along the grass verge.

A6033 LITTLEBOROUGH–TODMORDEN ROAD, BOTTOMLEY TO MANKINHOLES GR 941 208   3 MILES

Take the first turning sharp right onto a tarmac lane, Bottomley Road. Follow this lane between the cottages, and then right over the canal bridge. Go straight ahead between the houses onto the narrow stone-paved packhorse route that climbs steeply up to the hamlet of Bottomley. Go through the gate at the top of the hill, and then take the bridleway down the side of the third building on the left. Cross over the bridge and follow the packhorse route, now a stone causeway, all the way along until you come to a white house below on the left, Dean Royd Farm.

Here the packhorse route bears right up the hill to a small gate. After this gate ride along towards a white property on the right. Through a gate, you are now on a tarmac section of road, still the ancient highway. Follow this round to the next cluster of houses known as Hollingworth and at the junction bear right onto a narrow walled bridleway which takes you to the moor gate. "Highlands" on the right provides B&B for riders and the last house on the right has a **red telephone box** in the garden.

You are now on Salter Rake Gate, which will take you across Walsden Common around the shoulder of the hill, crossing the old Lancashire–Yorkshire boundary just before the crest of the hill, to drop down to the **Shepherd's Rest** public house. This old packhorse route was used for bringing salt from Cheshire in Saxon times. Note the groove worn in the old paving stones by the heavy use of shod packhorses over the years. On the last section, as the track passes between two walls, look for the Shurcrack milestone on the right, which marks the former ways to Rochdale, Burnley and Halifax (the track to Burnley has disappeared).

On reaching the road turn right and follow it for nearly a mile and as you come into Lumbutts Village, the road bends right. On the bend obscured by trees and bushes you will see another extremely narrow packhorse route on the left. (See map.)

Follow this uphill a short way and you will come out at the **Top Brink** public house. Go straight across the pub car park onto another narrow paved bridleway with a little milestone on the left. This marks the old road to Halifax and Heptonstall. The bridleway brings you out on the tarmac road in Mankinholes opposite the old Methodist Sunday school, now a house called Lane Head. (To reach Cross Farm B&B turn left along the highway.)

Lumbutts & Top Brink

Mankinholes is a very early settlement, but most of the stone buildings date from the 18th century, and have fine mullioned windows with drip courses. The prosperity of the yeoman farmers was based on the dual economy of agriculture and cloth. Wool (much of which was imported from other parts of the country) was spun and woven at home, and the outline of the 'takking in' doors can still be seen on some of the house walls. This door gave access up a flight of stone steps from the road direct to the upper storey where the weaving was done.

By contrast, Lumbutts is an early industrial village in character, and once boasted a school and a Co-op, which only closed in the 1960s. The village grew to provide the workforce for the four cotton mills powered by the stream in Lumbutts Clough. The square lower by the activities centre is all that remains of Lumbutts mill, which was built in the 1790s.

MANKINHOLES TO A646 TODMORDEN–HEBDEN BRIDGE ROAD GR 961 234   4¹/₂ MILES

Having turned right (the ancient highway turns left on its way to Hebden Bridge and Heptonstall) ride through the village passing the Youth Hostel on the left. At the end of the village, just after the series of water troughs, take the bridleway to the left. This is London Road, but the road to London no more. Through a gate it brings you onto Langfield Common and the bridleway continues on with the moor wall on the left. Above on the hill stands Stoodley Pike.

The stone obelisk on top of Stoodley Pike is the second monument to be built there. The first was put up in 1814 to mark the end of the Napoleonic wars, but fell down in 1854 at the outbreak of the Crimean War. A second (the present) monument was built in 1856, with some financial assistance from the Freemasons.

London Road leaves Langfield Common, and continues on as an open rough track to a farm at Swillington, then down a wide walled lane to a junction of tracks. At this point the route has now changed – if you want to visit the hamlet of Horsehold carry straight on past Kilnshaw Farm, but to stay on the PB, turn left at the cross roads. Follow the track down to a right hand turn on to a grassy track called Pinnacle Lane. At the end turn left through the gate and follow the new path down the hill to Callis Wood. At the bottom turn sharp left to the gate and the packhorse bridge over the stream. Follow this narrow path up the hill to join the farm road. After short distance turn right off the farm road to take a softer track through the trees, and after 400 yards or so re-join the farm road. Follow the road down the hill, through the sharp right hand bend in front of a house, then round a sharp left hand bend to a gate next to a cattle grid. Continue down the hill, over the canal bridge, then over the river bridge to the **Pegasus crossing** on the A646 Todmorden – Hebden Bridge road.

A646 Todmorden–Hebden Bridge Road to BADGER LANE, BLACKSHAW HEAD GR 971 264   2 MILES

Go straight across the road and turn left onto the new section of bridleway that runs parallel to the main road in front of a care home. At the end of the path turn right onto **Jumble Hole Road,** go under the railway bridge, pass the detached houses and start to climb the hill through the wood round a tight right-hand bend – Jumble Hole Clough stream and waterfall on the left. As the track starts to level out the PB turns off to the left, and climbs steeply round a sharp left-hand bend, then a sharp right-hand bend. At this point the path narrows until you come out at the top with a property called **Dove Scout Farm** on the left.

Once here, stop for a breather whilst you admire the view behind you. Congratulations – you have just climbed 650 feet! Turn right and follow the farm road gently up the hill to meet Badger Lane at the top. (B&B is provided at Badger Fields Farm – turn right for $^1/_4$ mile and the farm entrance is on the left.) To continue on the PB turn left on the road and take the first bridleway on the right next to Bracewell Hall Farm.

BADGER LANE, BLACKSHAW HEAD TO GORPLE LOWER RESERVOIR GR 964 275   5 MILES

Take the bridleway, Bow Lane, off Badger Lane in a northerly direction that heads up the hill between the houses. Bracewell Hall Farm is on the left. Go up the hill and down the other side and, as you descend, over to the right you can see Heptonstall church, in front of you the Colden valley, with the school to the left. At the bottom of the hill keep to the left of Shaw Bottom House to meet Shaw Bottom Lane, and turn left.

After 300 yards you meet a tarmac road, Shaw New Road. Turn left here (the New Delight pub is just below to the right). The PB follows the road up the hill to the next bend, a distance of about 500 yards. As the main road bends left take the farm road, Brown Hill Lane, in front of you and follow this track for $3/4$ mile to the last property, Strines Clough Farm, at the end of the lane. As you approach the yard the bridleway turns right along the field fence on a grass track leading down to a gate. Follow this section of bridleway, which crosses two streams and passes through several gates, until you come to a house surrounded by sycamore trees – ride along with the trees and two ponds on your right to cross a farm road. (See map.)

Go straight across through a gate into a field, bear slightly to the right and ride down the edge of the field with a wall on your right. Follow the path down through a gate, after which the track becomes a holloway called Sunderland Lane, which is part of a medieval road that crossed the Calder Valley to Erringden. Before the holloway there is a water trough on the left a few yards from the track. Through the gate at the bottom the track bends left with a house, Land Farm, with large colourful gardens below on your right. The gardens are open to the public during the summer months. At Land Farm the track continues ahead (a deep holloway takes off to the left at this point) to cross a bridge and then climbs up the hill on a tarmac lane to meet Edge Lane

Strines Clough & Sunderland Lane
Higher Colden

at a T-junction. (At this point the PB turns left, but there is a farm shop down the lane to the right, which sells home-made pies, sandwiches, and thirteen different types of champagne.)

Turn left on Edge Lane and ride along for nearly a mile past several farms and houses until you come to three gates in front of you. The two left-hand gates are private farm roads – take the right-hand gate onto the moor. Follow the track until you see **Gorple Lower Reservoir** below you and, over to the right, Walshaw Dean Lower and Middle Reservoirs. Ride down the hill through a horsestile and then through a wrought-iron gate onto a water board access road. Turn left to ride past a former water board house to the dam head.

GORPLE LOWER RESERVOIR TO HURSTWOOD RESERVOIR
GR 944 312   5 MILES

Ride across the dam and follow the track all the way down to
meet Halifax Road and turn left. Ride for $^3/_4$ mile along the road
to take the first bridleway off to the left at **Widdop Reservoir**.
The PB crosses the dam head and skirts the south side of the
reservoir before swinging southwest – this is Gorple Road, once
an important lime route between Halifax and Worsthorne.

Follow Gorple Road for 2 miles over the crest of the hill (some
425 metres above sea level) and the watershed between Yorkshire
and Lancashire. Once on Gorple Road take care not to stray from
the track as there are deep bogs. As you cross from Yorkshire back
into Lancashire, away to your left you can see Langfield Common
and Stoodley Pike, and round to the right Top of Leach, which at
474 metres is the highest point on the MTL. On a good day you
can see the purple hills of the Pennines stretching away south
into the distance, like so many great humpbacked whales. As
Hurstwood Reservoir comes into view take the bridleway that
forks off to the left over Hurstwood Brook.

HURSTWOOD RESERVOIR TO LONG CAUSEWAY,
COALCLOUGH GR 891 321   2 MILES

Ride along with the reservoir on your right until you come to
the dam wall, then follow the main track that turns left up the
hill. This track takes you down to **Cant Clough Reservoir** – ride
along the dam head to the far end and turn right. Follow this
track along and down the hill to a packhorse bridge – ride over
the bridge and turn left to the stream crossing. Note the series
of strange humps both sides of the track – these are the spoil
heaps from the lime-burning industry that occupied Shedden
several hundred years ago. The lime kilns, where the lime was
heated to separate it from the waste material, are long gone and
the spoil is all that remains.

Having crossed the stream, ride along with the stream on your
right and turn right, crossing the stream at the ford. At the top

of the incline cross another stream via a plank bridge, and turn first right. At the top of the rise you will see the **Long Causeway** in the distance.

The sandwiches come out at Widdop Reservoir

Hamlet of Horsehold C1920

Packponies carrying bolts of cloth on the ascent to the Nick of Pendle